A Red Fox Book

Published by Random House Children' s Books
20 Vauxhall Bridge Road, London SW1V 2SA

A division of Random House UK Ltd
London Melbourne Sydney Auckland
Johannesburg and agencies throughout the world

1 3 5 7 9 10 8 6 4 2

First published in Great Britain by Andersen Press Ltd

Red Fox edition 1999

Printed in Hong Kong

RANDOM HOUSE UK Limited Reg. No. 954009

ISBN 0 09 940037 5

J112 852
£4.99

GOLDFISH
HIDE·AND·SEEK

SATOSHI KITAMURA

Red Fox

Hello, Heidi. Let's play hide-and-seek!

You go and hide while I count to ten.
ONE...TWO...THREE...FOUR...FIVE...

...SIX...SEVEN...EIGHT...NINE...TEN!
Coming, ready or not!

Is she behind the rock? No…

Is she among the seaweed? No…

Miss Frog, have you seen Heidi?
"No, I'm too busy chiselling."

Fish, have you bumped into Heidi?
"No, she hasn't swum into our net."

Turtles, has Heidi come this way?
"No, we haven't checked her, mate."

Mr Octopus, have you seen Heidi?
   "No, I see nothing but my art."

Doctor Angler, have you spotted Heidi?
"No, she hasn't come to light."

Does anyone know where Heidi is?

I look everywhere…

Perhaps she's gone outside? I'll have a quick look…

Wow! I'm flying. This is exciting.

Uh-oh! Hello,
Mr Cat, how are you?
"Hungry."
Would you like
some seaweed?
I'll go home
and get it.

"I'm no vegetarian."
That's too bad!
Well, I feel like dancing.
Can you dance,
Mr Cat?

One, two, three… one, two, three… Left, right, left-right, left…

OOPS!

That's it, Mr Cat. You're not bad at all...

Heidi, there you are!

I've had enough of hide-and-seek.
Dancing is the thing. Let's dance…

Some bestselling Red Fox picture books

THE BIG ALFIE AND ANNIE ROSE STORYBOOK
by Shirley Hughes
OLD BEAR
by Jane Hissey
OI! GET OFF OUR TRAIN
by John Burningham
DON'T DO THAT!
by Tony Ross
NOT NOW, BERNARD
by David McKee
ALL JOIN IN
by Quentin Blake
THE WHALES' SONG
by Gary Blythe and Dyan Sheldon
JESUS' CHRISTMAS PARTY
by Nicholas Allan
THE PATCHWORK CAT
by Nicola Bayley and William Mayne
WILLY AND HUGH
by Anthony Browne
THE WINTER HEDGEHOG
by Ann and Reg Cartwright
A DARK, DARK TALE
by Ruth Brown
HARRY, THE DIRTY DOG
by Gene Zion and Margaret Bloy Graham
DR XARGLE'S BOOK OF EARTHLETS
by Jeanne Willis and Tony Ross
WHERE'S THE BABY?
by Pat Hutchins